V!SiONS

This book thanks all parents who like Bill and Dorothy Thompson, provided a fully functional environment that ultimately gave their children the freedom and confidence to be able to see and feel art both aural and visual, but specifically in word and fiber.

- Stevii Thompson Graves

Copyright ©1994 Quilt San Diego, 9747 Business Park Avenue, Suite 228, San Diego, California 92131

- Photography by Carina Woolrich, San Diego, California

- Front Cover Quilt: Detail of *Freehand 8: Torn* by Liz Axford, Houston, Texas

- Editing by Stevii Thompson Graves, San Diego, California

- Copy Editing by Louise Owens Townsend

- Technical Editing by Florence Stone

- Design and Production Coordination by Jill Maxwell Berry, Artista Artworks, San Diego, California

- Published by C&T Publishing, P.O. Box 1456, Lafayette, California 94549

- ISBN 0-914881-82-5

- Library of Congress Cataloging-in-Publication Data

Visions: quilts, layers of excellence /Stevii Thompson Graves, editor ; Quilt San Diego; [photography by Carina Woolrich].
    p. cm.
Catalog of an exhibition held at the Museum of San Diego History.
Includes index.
ISBN 0-914881-82-5
1. Quilts—United States—History—20th century— Exhibitions.
I. Graves, Stevii Thompson. II. Quilt San Diego (Organization). III. Museum of San Diego History.
NK9112.V58 1994
746.3973'09'049074794985—dc20   94-1203
                                        CIP

Printed in Hong Kong

5   4   3   2   1

VISIONS

QUILTS

LAYERS·OF·EXCELLENCE

Stevii Thompson Graves, Editor

QUILT SAN DIEGO

C&T Publishing

ACKNOWLEDGMENTS

■ The mission statement of Quilt San Diego states that it is a not-for-profit international arts organization dedicated to the promotion and appreciation of the quilt as art. Quilt San Diego is achieving its purpose by the establishment of a worldwide network of dedicated members, advisers, associates, and affiliates that

■ organize and stage exhibitions of outstanding quilts in museum quality settings,

■ present workshops, lectures, and related activities to its members, the world arts community, and the general public,

■ promote presentations and discussions of the quilt as art, and

■ encourage and promote quilting of the highest aesthetic and artistic quality.

In order to attain these goals, Quilt San Diego has assembled an invaluable team of supporters, mostly volunteer, that are vital to the success of the organization.

Special appreciation is given to:

■ Susan Knobloch, Executive Director of Quilt San Diego and her Assistant, Marilynn Wilde;

■ Members of the Quilt San Diego Board of Directors: Christen Brown, Alice Busse, Martha Ehringer, Shirley Grear, Barbara Hartung, Judy Hopkins, Janet Rogers, and Julie Zgliniec;

■ Former members of the Quilt San Diego Board of Directors: Diane Seaberg, Karen Emberton, Debby Timby, Patty Garretson, Shirlee Smith, Cynthia Hansen, Pat Marean, Lynn Johnson, Kate Besser, Carol O'Brien, Karen Wooten, Linda Hamby, Sharyn Craig, Arlene Stamper, Patty Smith, and Rose Turner;

■ Visions Committee Chairpersons: Arlene Stamper, Linda Hamby, Christen Brown, Thayes Hower, Susan Knobloch, Julie Zgliniec, Lee Ann Decker, Merilyne Hickman, Diane Stone, Dorie Refling, Harriet Love, Stevii Thompson Graves, Diane Seaberg, Lynn Johnson, and Judy Hopkins;

■ Our generous members, corporate sponsors, and the quilt lovers of San Diego;

■ The San Diego Historical Society and Lucinda Eddy; and

■ C&T Publishing: Managing Partners, Todd and Tony Hensley; Editorial Design Director, Diane Pedersen; Editor, Louise Owens Townsend; and Technical Editor, Florence Stone.

Quilt San Diego also wishes to thank the hundreds of quilt artists around the world for their interest in and support of the goals of Quilt San Diego.

■ Stevii Thompson Graves
President, Board of Directors
Quilt San Diego

5

INTRODUCTION

■ It is with great pleasure that the San Diego Historical Society presents Quilt San Diego's fourth juried exhibition, *Visions: Quilts, Layers of Excellence*. Our association with Quilt San Diego began some years ago with plans for *Visions—A New Decade*. That extraordinary exhibition resulted in record attendance for our Museum of San Diego History in 1990 and the beginning of a successful collaboration between our two organizations. In 1992, the San Diego Historical Society was again honored to be the selected site for Quilt San Diego's third international juried exhibition, *Visions: The Art of the Quilt*. Today, we look forward to another collaboration and the opportunity to work with a group that has consistently organized and produced exhibitions of exceptional quality, diversity, and beauty.

■ The San Diego Historical Society was founded in 1928 to collect, preserve, and interpret the historical record of greater San Diego to the public. The Society's mission to document our region's history through exhibitions and publications is in many ways not unlike that of organizations such as Quilt San Diego whose biennial exhibitions and catalogs have recorded for future generations the contemporary art quilting movement of the 1980s and 1990s.

■ As San Diego's largest historical agency, we strive to present an accurate and insightful interpretation of the diverse peoples who have influenced the development of our city and county through the material culture, photographic images, and written testimonies they have left behind. In a very similar fashion, the *Visions* exhibitions, through the medium of quilts, have brought to light a rich tapestry of cultural influences, which say much about our contemporary society. Through fabric and thread, modern-day quilters infuse their work with social commentary, using design, color, and a host of innovative techniques to make bold political and social statements that are direct responses to today's complex and controversial issues. These quilts also frequently reveal a great deal about their makers. We see quilts that convey a wide range of emotions, from humor and joy to disillusionment, grief, and loss. Others depict the psychological journeys taken toward greater self-knowledge. Such quilts become intensely personal testimonies of self-discovery and fulfillment.

■ The *Visions* quilts clearly demonstrate new approaches being taken in the field of quiltmaking and may well challenge some viewers' more traditional concepts of the medium. The diversity of materials used, surface design elements, and construction techniques are just a few of the ways these quilt artists have chosen to stretch the rules, which have historically bound quiltmaking. A number of pieces amaze and even startle one with their similarity to abstract paintings. It is almost as though the eye has been tricked into seeing a painting on canvas and not a quilt. Undoubtedly, this exhibition will engender some controversy and raise more than a few eyebrows, but certainly it will also illustrate the breadth, vitality, creativity, and skill of today's quilt artists.

■ We invite you to share the energy and imagination these quiltmakers have brought to this enduring and beautiful art form and to celebrate with us its bright future.

■ Lucinda L. Eddy
Assistant Director of Museums
Curator, Museum of San Diego History
San Diego Historical Society

JURYING PHILOSOPHY

■ We define a work of art as a work that is in some way extraordinary. It is expressive and invites us to see ourselves and the world anew or inspires us in a new way.

■ We want the best in quiltmaking today. It is certainly not our intention to simply shock the public. While it is important to represent the range of today's quiltmaking, it is equally important that each quilt possess a vitality of its own and be able to stand alone as well as work together with the other quilts to provide an exhibition that somehow "gels" together.

■ We want the public to see a range of quilts, some that perhaps may initially "feel" familiar and also those that will make them stop and think, evoke an emotion, create an opinion. We want quilts that derive from the necessity to communicate—that speak from the soul of the quiltmaker.

■ We want quilts that flow with color, sparkle with excitement, those that make visual impacts, and those that are so subtle that one must look closely to see unusual use of fabric, high technical skills, and other marvelous effects used to create the design.

■ We want all those wonderful, incredible quilts that express the quiltmaker's creativity. We want an exhibit that compels the viewer to return for more than one look.

9

JUROR'S STATEMENT

■ Why did I choose the works that I chose? The truth is that I had no specific objective or subjective criteria in mind as I began to view the 905 entries. I entered the jurying process with heart and mind open, determined only to let the submitted works tell me what to do.

■ My initial responses were immediate and varied: nothing new; overcomplicated; no structure; compelling; strong color; weak concept; bad slide—can't read it; nothing beyond surface; silly theme; potent message; artless; unique technique but nothing more; interesting combination of techniques and materials; trying too hard to be "art"; seen a thousand times already; no energy, lackluster; commanding, authoritative; imitative; ordinary; lacks integrity; has integrity.

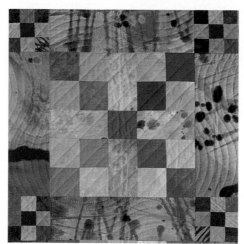

■ These and many other reactions filled my thoughts as I ran through all of the submissions and, in the second round, began eliminations. In short order, the field was narrowed down to some 100 entries, and the challenge of making difficult choices began.

■ Anyone who has juried a show from slides knows the process is hardly scientific. The reality of the projected slide image is never equivalent to the reality of the object itself. Inevitably, a few of my choices appear misguided to some, and I have only this explanation to offer. As I wrapped up the jurying for the exhibition, I remained less than 100% convinced about a handful of selections, and second thoughts wasted no time in beginning their discomforting mindplay. Taken as a whole, however, the 45 works seem to provide a substantive answer to the questions, "What's going on in the world of innovative quilts now?" and "What's important at this point in time for people to see?"

■ It's difficult to say what made the difference for me in the final selection rounds, when 100 or so quilts were narrowed down to 45, or 5% of the original total. For some reason, one quilt may have seemed to me to go just a bit further beyond the familiar or the predictable than another. I felt that some quilts had a sure-footedness and naturalness that others didn't display. In certain cases, color seemed to be employed with less self-consciousness. In others, techniques stepped out of the limelight in deference to the overall image and concept. These factors distinguished many of the final choices from their close seconds.

■ A number of entrants deserve special mention. Risë Nagin's *Target: On the Beach* and her work in general shine with refinement, authority, elegance, and impeccable workmanship. The marriage of imagery and symbolism to materials and techniques in her work defines, for me, what I mean when I use the word *integrity* in qualifying a contemporary quilt. Similarly, Emily Richardson's works orchestrate formal, expressive, and technical elements with such finesse and subtlety that their integrity is equally undeniable.

■ Mimi Holmes's *Quilt for the Death of One I Love(d) (Compost Quilt)* is simultaneously bizarre, touching, amusing, disturbing, depressing, and inspiring—a complicated piece about complicated emotions, inventively conceived and executed. Nancy Condon's *Bitches, Victims, Saints, and Whores One: Boundary Violations* takes another complicated theme and gives it a powerful visual reality that is neither over-embellished nor one-dimensionally political. Seen at a removed distance, it's a figure rendered with authority and grace. Up close, where the message is apparent, it becomes provocative and challenging.

■ Recognized quilt artists such as Linda MacDonald, Jan Myers-Newbury, Terrie Mangat, and Therese May are represented by new pieces from their ongoing work that reconfirm their mastery of the visual vocabularies and technical processes on which their reputations have been established. At the same time, emerging artists like Melissa Holzinger give the viewer, through their work, reason to look forward to the ongoing evolution and development of the non-traditional quilt form.

■ *Visions: Quilts, Layers of Excellence* would be a somewhat different exhibition had the selections been made by the usual committee of three jurors. I don't believe, however, that it would be significantly different. Cream rises to the top, and, consequently, I believe that most of the work shown here would have survived the negotiations of a panel of jurors.

■ Having participated in numerous juryings, however, I know firsthand that selection by committee inevitably requires compromises and that the impact of the resulting exhibition is diluted. I did not have to make compromises in selecting these works. I did not have to barter or plead or persuade in order to keep or to eliminate particular entries. This is not to say that making the final selections was any easier. They were made, however, against the background of one observer's 20 years of intimate association with and understanding of the world of contemporary quilts and fabric art. I understand that for Quilt San Diego to invite a single juror required a considerable degree of trust, and I hope they feel that trust was well placed.

■ The Quilt San Diego team that organized *Visions: Quilts, Layers of Excellence* deserves the appreciation of every entrant as well as every viewer of this exhibition. They have mine. Their efforts, largely volunteer, to provide a showcase for some of the most inventive work being done in this medium are a gift to the quilt world. For that they are to be applauded.

■ Michael James

Michael James holds B.F.A. and M.F.A. degrees in Painting and Printmaking, and his own work in quilts has developed out of this background. His work is included in the collections of the American Craft Museum and the Newark (New Jersey) Museum, as well as in numerous corporate and private collections. He has been awarded numerous fellowships for his work, including several from the National Endowment for the Arts. He lectures and teaches widely, and keeps up a steady production of quilts from his Somerset, Massachusetts, studio.

◆◆◆◆THE◆QUILTS◆◆◆◆

Target: On the Beach is one in a series of works in which my intention is to employ complex surfaces to evoke states of mind: Fleeting epiphanies, which float into our collective consciousness in an instant of recognition and then retreat to be forgotten.

[Editor's Note: This quilt is the 1994 Quilts Japan Awardee.]

RISË NAGIN
Pittsburgh, Pennsylvania

TARGET: ON THE BEACH
99.5" x 80.5"

Silk, cotton, polyester, rayon/nylon blend, acrylic paint, thread

Layered, stained, pieced, appliquéd, quilted, hand-sewn

SUSAN SHIE AND JAMES ACORD
Wooster, Ohio

NIGHT CHANT—A GREEN QUILT
63" x 76"

Fabric, Deka® paint, acrylic paint, leather, glass, beads, gemstones, bone carvings, polyclay

Hand-quilted, machine-quilted, embroidered, appliquéd, leather-tooled, painted, hand and air-brushed

Night Chant celebrates the Higher Self and our connection to this inner teacher as well as the ways in which people gain access to their intuitive souls. The crocodile in the lower center is fabric from an Ashanti mud cloth altered with quilted embellishment. Susan writes on the quilts after meditation and simply lets it come out. The first draft is on the piece. Glow-in-the-dark paint makes this quilt a lively experience at night—makes you feel like chanting and telling ghost stories! We feel a strong connection with the Voices Within, which help in healing us and thus in healing the Earth. Written instructions are for the writer and the viewer. We need encouragement to un-program our sophisticated, logical thinking to open up to our joyful spirits! This quilt is best experienced to the accompaniment of uplifting rhythmic music (drums and rattles) in the dark!

As when one looks up at the sky through a curtain of tree branches and leaves, this view continually shifts the focus between texture and color. Through the grid pattern, made from raw-edged canvas, the colors of painted cloth vary as do those of the sky with its windblown clouds and changing sun. *Sky Scape* is a moment caught in a frame, undoubtedly influenced by my urban surroundings.

EMILY RICHARDSON
Philadelphia, Pennsylvania

SKY SCAPE
30" x 35"

Acrylic and textile ink on canvas, muslin, string

Hand-appliquéd, machine-pieced, hand-quilted

18

ELLEN OPPENHEIMER
Oakland, California

ARI'S MAZE
46" x 46"
Commercial cottons
Machine-pieced, hand-quilted

My lesbian lover and I are the proud mothers of a wonderful baby named Ari. I started this quilt while I was pregnant with Ari. I did not want to use any inks or dyes while I was pregnant and so I started working on some designs using commercial fabrics that I had. As my pregnancy progressed, the designs kept getting more complicated, confused, and more impossible to conceive. About three weeks before my due date, I abandoned months of drawing and planning and put together a very reasonable and simple design, which I was able to start sewing before I went into labor. I finished this quilt in the first few months of our son Ari's life. He has been a great joy in my lover Carol's and my life.

There are six inner child quilts in this series. Each one has three flying saucers across the top made up of small painted panels, buttons, and beads. The flying saucers represent the bringing of great light. Each quilt also has a small narrow panel of zebra pattern fabric, which represents a time zone between Heaven and Earth. "Zeb," representing male energy, has birds and snakes flanking his head, a fish for a nose, and a fish above his head. He is responsive and shows great confidence.

THERESE MAY
San Jose, California

CHILD #1
30" x 41"
Fabric, paint, buttons, beads
Machine-appliquéd, beaded, painted

CYNTHIA CORBIN
Ben Lomond, California

SHADOW BOXING
54" x 54"

Cottons, Debra Lunn tie-dyed cottons, Marimekko cottons, cotton batting

Machine-pieced, machine-quilted

Shadow Boxing is part of a series in which I was exploring complexity within simple shapes—and I learned to get out of the way and let the fabric do its job. The Debra Lunn tie-dyes were the initial inspiration, and the alternate blocks mimic their pattern. At one point, this quilt was bordered in a completely different way. It was one of those things that looks good for about a day and a half—then you look at it again and think you've lost your mind. After much soul searching, I ripped it out. The quilt sat for several months. Two Marimekko fabrics jumped me one day in San Francisco. I recognized them—I had my border.

Machine quilting this one was a joy. It was an exploration in texturing a surface, and using the thread line as another design element.

This quilt was created for my grandmother, Sophia Antoinette Mayer Trastour, born in 1902 on the Isle of Cuba Plantation in Louisiana. At 91 she is still going strong, but her health is in decline. I made this quilt to help prepare myself for her eventual passing. At 37, I have not lost anyone close to me; people seem immortal within my immediate realm. Intellectually I know that people die, but emotionally I haven't quite accepted this fact as applying to my family.

The quilt is small, intended to be placed over her body in the coffin. I was thinking about quilts and how historically quilts were made by older women for births and weddings and keeping children and families warm. I wanted to turn that around and have a younger life make a quilt for an older death. I also wanted to make a quilt that wouldn't last, but was meant to decompose.

MIMI HOLMES
Minneapolis, Minnesota

QUILT FOR THE DEATH OF ONE I LOVE(D) (COMPOST QUILT)
34" x 60"

Obi stiffener fabric, netting, leather, wood, paint, zippers, thread, egg shells, dryer lint, vermiculite, dried coffee grounds, orange rinds, banana skins, grapefruit rind, fake horsehair (upholstery material), spray paint, copper

Fabric-dyed, machine-embroidered, machine-stitched, hand-stitched, hand-appliquéd

22

EMILY RICHARDSON
Philadelphia, Pennsylvania

JOURNEY—LOST/FOUND
53" x 53"

Textile ink on cotton muslin, silk, other fabrics

Hand-appliquéd, hand-embroidered

The process of my work is based on making parts and assembling or building these parts into a whole. While this piece is ultimately true to that process, it was conceived quite differently. I began by making a large painting on muslin using textile inks. Guided by my responses to the painting, I developed it using layers of stained sheer fabrics and other painted pieces including parts of the painting itself, which I had cut away. Although many images are suggested, the piece is meant to represent only the general concept indicated by the title: the range of experiences that a journey holds—from the uneasiness of darkness to the security of light—*Journey—Lost/Found.*

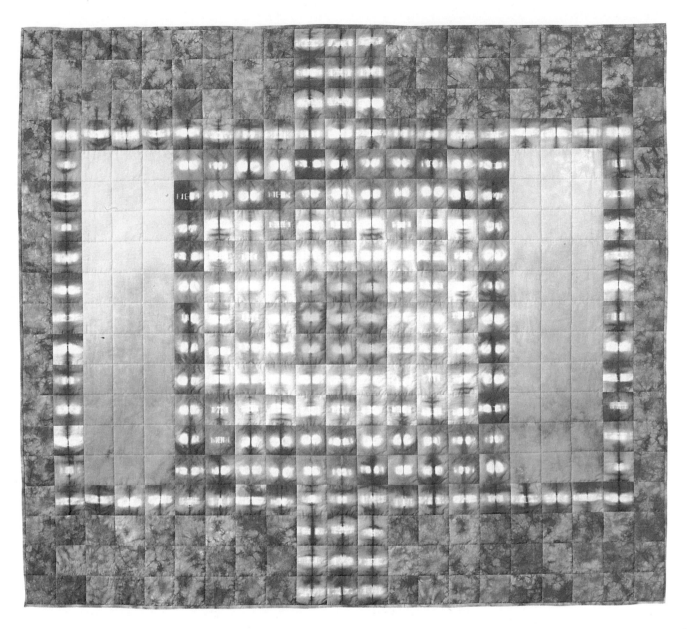

Recently various elements of pattern in my tie-dyed fabric have become the "alpha" of a design. Seldom do I know what the "omega" will be. The resist marks created by plastic clothespins on folded fabric have often suggested eyes to me. Repeating these eyes a hundred-fold was the starting point for this piece. They form a vague repeat pattern when viewed from a distance, but each pair of eyes is unique. The two vertical columns add a monumental quality to the intimacy of the forest of eyes; they also make the scale of the work ambiguous, which I like.

JAN MYERS-NEWBURY
Pittsburgh, Pennsylvania

SEEING IS BELIEVING
52" x 47"
Tie-dyed cottons
Tie-dyed, machine-pieced, machine-quilted

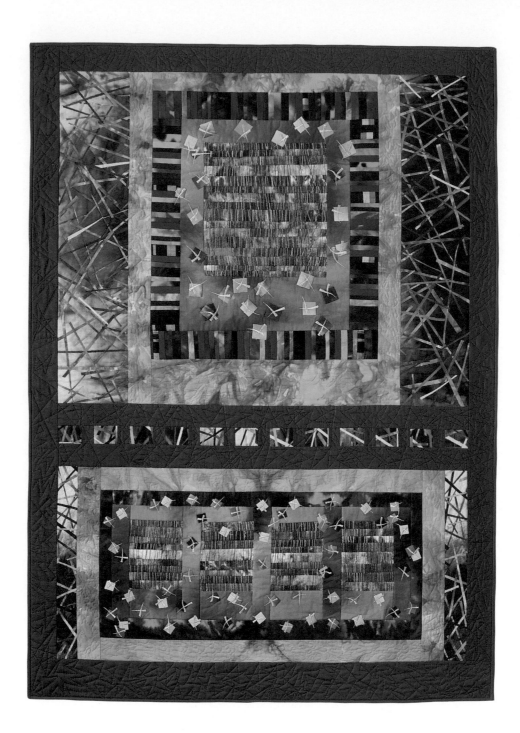

MELODY JOHNSON
Cary, Illinois

VAULT OF KEPT PROMISES
41" x 57"

Commercial and hand-dyed
(Procion® MX) cottons and silks,
hand-dyed perle cotton thread,
metallic thread

Heat-bond appliquéd, machine-
embroidered, machine-pieced,
machine-quilted

In making my art I am often thwarted by the voice
in my head, which I call "The Inhibitor." This voice
is cautious, avoids risks, and obeys rules. If I listen to
this voice, I make safe art. Instead I try to tune in to
the voice of "The Encourager," who promises me
that if I take the chance, if I try reaching a little
higher, I might break through the walls of safety and
make something wonderful. I believe in that
promise.

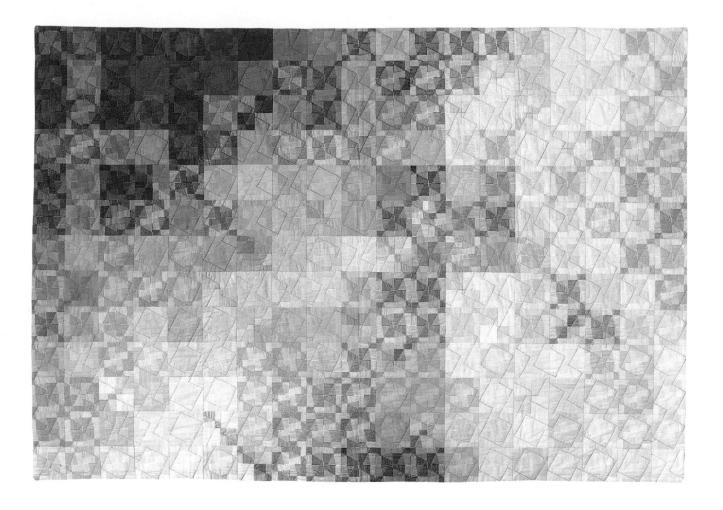

Living in the Pacific Northwest on the edge of the
continent, the expansiveness of sky and the opportunity to watch its rapid changes are daily events for
me. I particularly love sunsets over the Olympic
Mountains and Puget Sound. The intensity of color
plus the ephemeral nature of the event (look away
for a minute or two, and the patterns have shifted)
are a metaphor for me of life's passion and the certainty of change. Those sunsets and a heartstopping
sunrise in Bali inspired the color and sense of movement in *Solar Palette*.

KAREN N. SOMA
Seattle, Washington

SOLAR PALETTE
75" x 52"

Cotton fabrics, fiber-reactive dyes,
fabric pigments, metallic threads

Hand-dyed fabrics, hand screen-
printed motifs, machine-pieced,
machine-quilted, machine-
embroidered

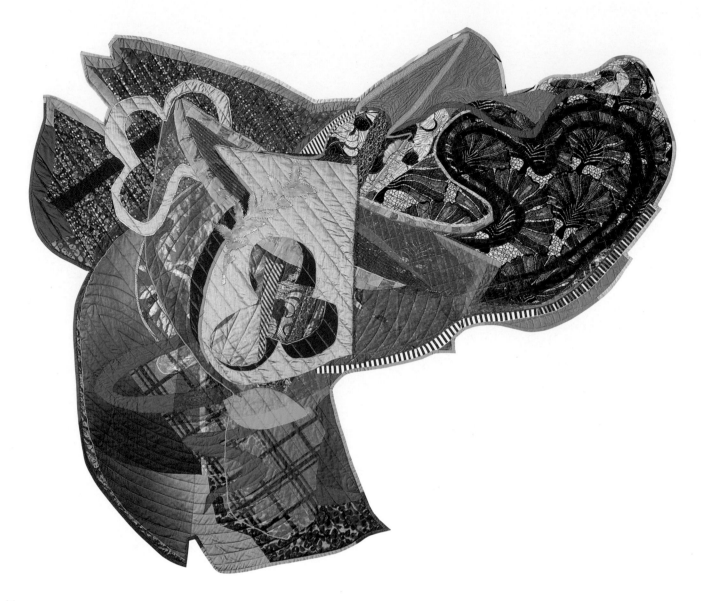

KATHLEEN O'CONNOR
Putney, Vermont

ACE OF CUPS
98" x 96"

Hand-dyed cottons, silk, acrylic paint, plastic, embroidery floss, cotton and rayon thread

Appliquéd, hand-dyed and painted fabric, machine-embroidered, machine-quilted

In 1993 a client commissioned me to "make whatever you want to make next." Wonderful client—good fun. *Ace of Cups* is one of a group of "shapely" pieces kicked off by that commission. Flying forms often occur in my work. With this body of work, I allowed the whole piece to fly.

The Ace of Cups is a tarot card that signifies abundance, harmony, and creativity. Happy things to contemplate or to build a quilt around.

In my Dwellings series, I am concerned with structures, focusing on their geometrical interest as well as their emotional content. I am enamored of the image of a house as children see it: First, draw it—joyful, uneven triangles and squares and rectangles. I use this image over and over again. In *The Neighborhood*, I yielded again to this fascination and explored the quirky differences, which endear houses and their inhabitants to me.

SALLY A. SELLERS
Vancouver, Washington

THE NEIGHBORHOOD
64" x 51.5"

Cottons, synthetic fabrics

Machine-appliquéd, machine-pieced, machine-quilted

28

GAYLE A. PRITCHARD
Bay Village, Ohio

MASKS II: THE JOYBRINGER
33" x 23"

Cotton and blends, silk organza, hand-dyed fabrics, string, yarn, embroidery floss, violin strings, buttons, beads, acrylic paint, metallic thread

Machine-pieced, machine-appliquéd, hand-quilted, machine-quilted, painted, embellished

The second in the Masks series, this quilt was influenced by tribal art as well as the religious triptych tradition. Like a prayer rug, this is a place to find spiritual renewal, peace, meditation. My work has been exploring these themes during and after a series of losses. Through my work I have been able to find grounding.

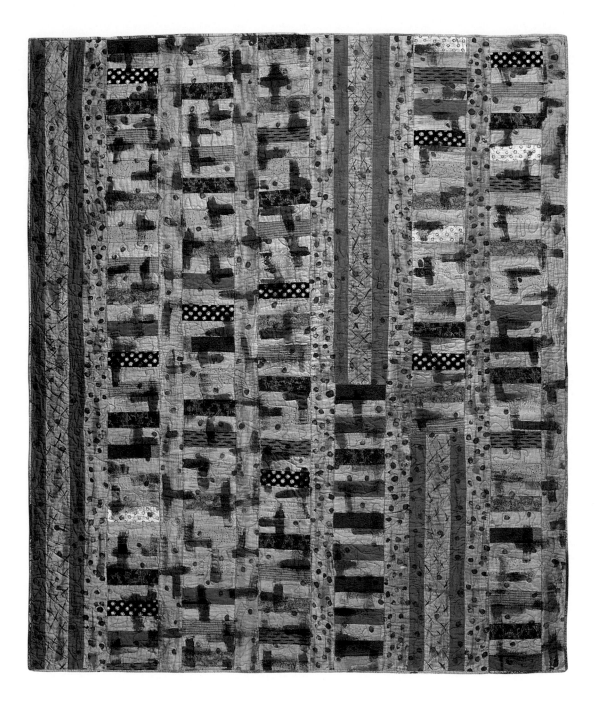

The origins of this quilt lie in the art of antique scrap quilting. I have long been attracted to the challenge of making a unified whole from a set of available scraps while remaining true to my own artistic temperament. The inspiration that finally provided the glue for bringing these complementary demands together was a recollection of the frequent use of the color combination of indigo and persimmon in Japanese art. This finally allowed me to integrate scraps with my own voice.

SUZAN FRIEDLAND
San Francisco, California

INDIGO AND PERSIMMON
67" x 80"

Cotton, silk, linen, Warm and Natural™ batting

Hand-painted, machine-pieced, machine-quilted

BARBARA OTTO
Lake Elmo, Minnesota

**HOME SERIES: ROTE DÄCHER
(RED ROOFS)**
91" x 70"

Cotton muslin, commercial cotton,
Procion® H series dyes, polyester
batting

Hand-painted with thickened
Procion® H dyes, wax resist,
machine-quilted

This work has sources in both fine art and fine craft.
Swiss artist Paul Klee's landscapes provide inspiration as does the tradition of American pieced quilts.
The simple geometric shapes used are common to
both. Red triangles suggest abstract roofs on imagi-
nary houses, which remind me of the red roofs of
German towns.

My primary desire and challenge underlying my
recent work has been to explore drawing and painting directly on fabric. Other concerns encompassed
in this exploration included the wish to move
beyond the pieced-quilt approach, a desire to focus
on the process and materials of choice, and the fin-
ishing of the work as "quilts," which included
employing the stitching line as a secondary element
to the painted and drawn images. Fiber, in the form
of the quilt, is still my medium of choice, but I wish
to blur the distinction between quilting and
painting.

The two pieces of cloth used for this quilt were painted in October 1992. Ann Johnston taught me the basic techniques for dye painting. She encouraged experimentation with a variety of tools so I nonchalantly dabbed with a sponge brush and assorted found objects. Soon the cloth was dotted with the exuberance of autumn, and I was engrossed in the colors and patterns that emerged. It was already spring when I cut the fabric and actually made the quilt. There was no plan for the cutting, piecing, or quilting. I worked intuitively. After the quilt was finished, I decided to call it *Indian Summer* as I remembered the joy of autumn sunshine and color in a time of clear crisp air before winter's challenges.

While *Indian Summer* was in process, I had my 50th birthday. To me, midlife is like Indian summer: One must seize each day's possibilities and make the most of all the bright spots.

BARBARA MOLL
Muncie, Indiana

INDIAN SUMMER
40" x 39"

Cotton (hand-painted using sponge brushes and found objects, dyed with Procion® Fiber Reactive dye), polyester batting

Machine-pieced, hand-quilted; white binding by Mary McGhee

SUE BENNER
Dallas, Texas

FOUR PATCH I: JUNE BACKYARD
86" x 105"

Hand-dyed fabrics by Sue Benner,
Leslie Morgan, Debra Lunn, and
Nancy Crow, commercial cottons,
cotton batting, cotton thread

Direct application and immersion-
dyed (dye on cotton, dye-painted)
with fiber-reactive dyes, machine-
pieced, hand-quilted by Julie
Barnes

My studio windows overlook my backyard, a somewhat unkempt scene almost completely canopied by
mature elm, oak, and pecan trees. As the seasons
change, I often record in my work the changing
color and light I see. One June during the height of
Dallas greenness, I began to dye and paint fabric
using as many values and hues of green as I could
mix, trying to match the view of my backyard.
Intending to make a quilt that was semi-representa-
tional, I later chose the framework of a traditional
Amish Four Patch with sashing and Nine Patch
inserts. I arranged the light and shadow in the four
patches to imitate the dappled sunlight coming
through the trees. The hot hues of red, magenta, and
orange were my hopes that my impatiens would
bloom and thrive in the shady vista.

After reading Natalie Goldberg's *Writing Down the Bones*, an inspirational book on creative writing, I decided to try to translate some of her creative writing exercises into visual terms. The purpose of the exercises was to promote a more spontaneous, less judgmental approach to my work. After completing a number of "exercise blocks," I decided to assemble some of them into a larger quilt. I used a hand-painted canvas as background and attached the blocks with large stitches as was consistent with the nature of the blocks.

DIANA BUNNELL
Boulder, Colorado

SEWING DOWN THE BONES
55.5" x 69"

Cotton, hand-painted canvas, fabric dyes and paint, acrylic paint, threads, yarn

Machine-pieced, machine-quilted, hand-tied, hand-sewn

LINDA R. MACDONALD
Willits, California

SOFT METALS
56" x 53"

Cotton print cloth, acrylic paints, metallic paints, quilting thread, heavy-duty thread, cotton batting

Hand-dyed, airbrushed, hand-painted, machine-sewn, hand-sewn

Metal, pressed metal grids, light/dark contrast, the hard edge, the slick, the tucked and pleated, the shiny, the dull, corrosion upon the slick and shiny, chance occurrences of stain and color—I am fascinated by this. Airborne droplets of paint applied with a commercial art tool (airbrush) create the metal illusions. Experimental dyeing techniques create the chance and irregular field. The patterned regular grid is spattered with the chance image of the field. I like to explore and, I hope, to enhance the drama between the two.

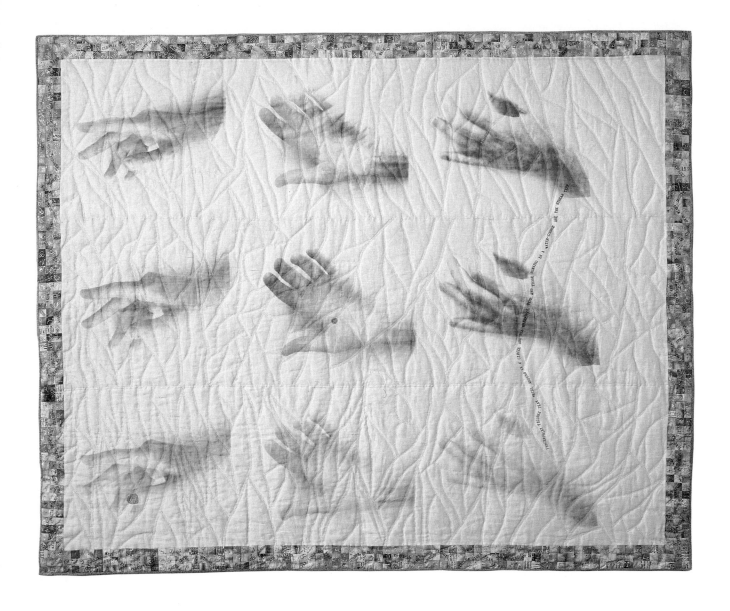

"Throughout history, palm-readers have chosen the hand as their symbolic link to the psyche and soul, as their raft through time. After all, the hand is action, it digs roads and builds cities, it throws spears and diapers babies." (Excerpt from *A Natural History of the Senses* by Diane Ackerman, Vintage Books/Division of Random House, New York, 1990, pg. 116)

RACHEL BRUMER
Seattle, Washington

TENTED ARCHES, WHORLS, AND SWOOPS
66" x 78"

Linen, Debra Lunn hand-dyed fabrics, plexi-foil, fabric sensitizer, polyester batting

Contact-printed, stamped, machine-pieced, hand-quilted

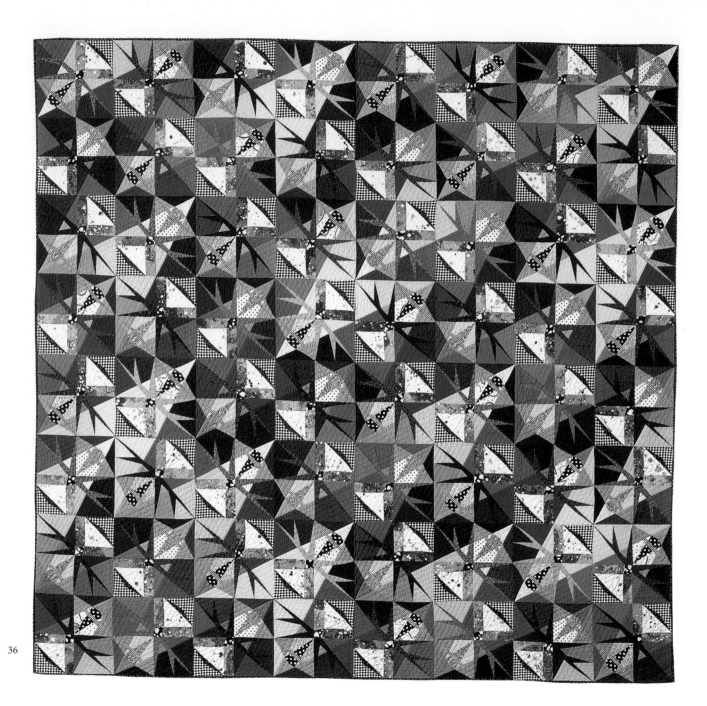

SHARON HEIDINGSFELDER
Little Rock, Arkansas

MOONGEM OF PARADISE
80" x 80.5"
Cotton fabrics
Dyed fabric, machine-pieced,
machine-quilted

Full Spectrum was commissioned by P&B Textiles to demonstrate the range and beauty of their solid-color cotton fabric. I used 95 of the approximately 105 solids currently available from P&B. The challenge was to find a way to use colors together that ranged from full chroma and intensity to very soft tints and very grayed tones of the color wheel. I clustered colors into color families and accented the main colors with complementary colors. I grouped the most intense colors in the center spokes and placed the less intense, paler colors on the outer edges. Black was used in angled "veins" to give drama, focus, and unity to the composition. The "image" of this quilt is very loosely based on the idea of flowers in a bouquet.

JUDITH LARZELERE
Belmont, Massachusetts

FULL SPECTRUM
58" x 58"

Ninety-five colors of P&B Textiles cotton solids

Machine strip-pieced, machine strip-quilted

JANE DUNNEWOLD
San Antonio, Texas

THE HEALING HEART
48" x 67"

Dyed rayon, commercial velvet,
commercial satin

Silk-screened with paint and foiled,
edges burned, machine-quilted

My Heart series of quilts was inspired by a painful
year of trying to reconcile the facts of finally growing
up at 39, with the fantasy of adolescent expectations.
Making quilts helped me bear the load I had to carry
at that time. *The Healing Heart* may be the end of
the series. Creating it was a celebratory experience
that had to do with many things—acknowledging
strength, choosing responsibility and trust, and
learning how to truly forgive. It is important to me
that my six-year-old daughter, Zenna, be acknowl-
edged as the maker of the heart image in the quilt.
Her example has opened the doors that led to my
own healing.

In my work I often find myself turning to imagery remembered from childhood. Most recently I've worked with Christian iconography taken from "holy cards" I received as a child in the 1950s. These images were potent ones for me as a young girl; as a skeptical adult, I conjure them up with a mixture of yearning and irony. Secondhand household textiles—garments, curtains, table linens—from the time when I believed in the myths and symbols of the Catholic pantheon are my primary source of material. I find joy in the process of creating relationships out of materials gleaned from many sources, salvaged on their way out of one family's life and into a creative piece. I also find humor in these transformations (tablecloth into mantle, skirt into halo) and hope the viewer does also.

MARY CATHERINE LAMB
Portland, Oregon

GUADALUPE REPERCEIVED
72" x 108"

Secondhand household fabrics, commercial satins, and metallics, photo transfers

Machine-appliquéd, machine-pieced, hand-quilted

JEAN NEBLETT
San Francisco, California

ABSTRACTION II: BLUE COLUMN
37" x 48"

Hand-dyed cottons by Eric Morti
and Debra Lunn, commercial cottons, silk chiffon

Torn, machine-appliquéd,
machine-quilted, scrimmed

Simplicity of form is explored through placement
and the use of scrim in this quilt of torn fabric.

The development of planes is explored in this quilt of torn and folded fabric through the use of placement and form, color and scrim.

JEAN NEBLETT
San Francisco, California

ABSTRACTION V: FIELD OF YELLOW
49" x 49"

Hand-dyed cottons by Nancy Crow, Eric Morti, and Debra Lunn, commercial cotton, netting, ribbon

Torn, folded, machine-appliquéd, machine-quilted, scrimmed

DORLE STERN-STRAETER
Munich, Germany

STUDY IN GREEN
68" x 65"

Cotton, silk, hand-dyed fabrics

Machine-pieced, hand-quilted
using the artist's own "crazy
technique"

Since 1988, I have been working off and on with this
particular block in a kite-form. First I divided it into
a Nine Patch, then in several different patterns. In
this piece, the block is used by dividing the tessellated
kite-form once horizontally and once vertically. This
gives me a diagonal division, which I worked from
dark to light in my own crazy technique.

The interaction of colors, the contrast of textures, the relationship between shapes and lines, the formal elements of visual art and the reactions, intellectual and emotional, which they can elicit in the viewer— these are the aspects of quiltmaking that interest me most.

Structural Inconsistencies is the first in a new series of quilts, but it builds on the work in earlier series. Clear, bright colors, wedge-shaped pieces, and overlapping grids have been part of previous quilts. The new element in *Structural Inconsistencies* is the erratic strip piecing. It grew out of a suggestion by Nancy Crow that one could set aside all the straight line tools and cut fabric freehand, just as one draws or paints freehand. What a liberating notion!

In making quilts I am always striving to create energetic, complex images which call the viewer back for another look.

RUTH GARRISON
Tempe, Arizona

STRUCTURAL INCONSISTENCIES
58" x 59"

Cotton fabrics, cotton/polyester batting

Machine-pieced, machine-quilted

MEINY VERMAAS-VAN DER HEIDE
Tempe, Arizona

EARTH QUILT #20: SOUTHWEST VI
81.5" x 51"

Cotton fabrics, Mountain Mist®
Cotton Choice batting

Machine-pieced, machine-quilted

44

I view each of my quilts as a challenge that satisfies my hunger for beauty, color, form, and texture. This quilt has been inspired by Piet Mondriaan's studies in line and color as well as the colors of the Southwest. *Earth Quilt #20: Southwest VI* explores positive/negative in design and image, simultaneous contrast, as well as color perception and manipulation within the quilt surface. The abstracter the image, the better I like it. Art should make visible the invisible from within. This is true for the maker as well as for the viewer. It is irrelevant when the visible is something different for everyone: The artwork is the mediator, the focal point enabling the viewer to let the mind wander.

At the same time I want to share emotion in my quilts, whether religious, personal, or universal. Many of my quilts are labeled as "Green Quilts" or "Earth Quilts." "Earth Quilts" are my acknowledgment that environmental issues cannot be seen without questioning "war and peace," economic, and social issues as well. The definition of "Earth Quilts" is wider and can include "Green Quilts." The charge in Genesis to be "stewards of the earth" is my inspiration for making these quilts, which I feel is my vocation as a Christian.

Of all the seasons, summer seems to encompass the most positive feelings and turning points of one's life. This quilt was conceived as the sentiment and memory of one's past summer. It is composed of an arrangement of cloth pictures. Framed images that are painted and stitched overlap and intertwine as do the variations and complexities of my recollection of last summer.

EMILY RICHARDSON
Philadelphia, Pennsylvania

LAST SUMMER
36" x 66"

Acrylic on silk, cotton, linen, other assorted fabrics, cotton yarn, string

Hand-appliquéd, hand-embroidered, hand-quilted

TERRIE HANCOCK MANGAT
Cincinnati, Ohio

HANCOCK MEMORIAL QUILT
83" x 114"

Cotton, novelty cloth, oil-painted canvas, beads, acrylic-sealed paper images, embroidery thread, acrylic paint, photo silk-screened images

Machine-appliquéd, reverse-appliquéd, embroidered, painted, strip-pieced, cut throughs, beaded, silk-screened, quilted by Sue Rule

The *Hancock Memorial Quilt* is a memorial to my mom and dad. After the wreck, my sister Becky and I wanted to put one of those New Mexico crosses on the roadside, but instead I put the crosses on a quilt.

The crosses are on a mound made of an old Grandmother's Flower Garden quilt with grandchildren's names embroidered on the flowers. By my dad's cross are embroidered dog trophies because he raised beagles, and grocery items and coins because he sold groceries and collected coins. On my mom's cross is a wreath made of an old embroidered table-cloth embellished with her jewelry because she loved a festive house. Around her cross are cooking utensils because she cooked well for many.

Mary is quite large between the crosses. Mom was very religious and knew that Mary was to appear at their parish church and that she wouldn't be there for it.

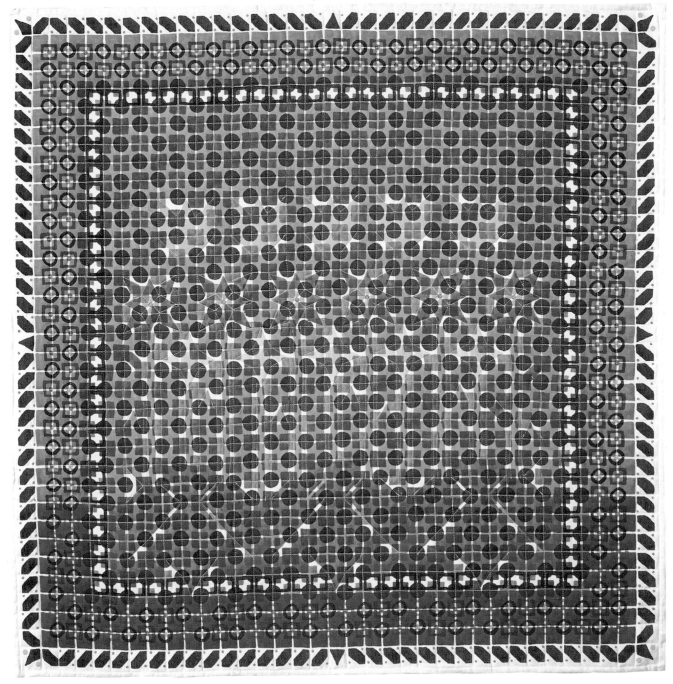

Every year as winter is slowly winding down and spring is trying to make its way to New England, I always enjoy going to the Flower Show. It is a time to remember that I will eventually have time to play outside in my garden. While weaving through the crowd, I can never get over the fact that the flowers at the Flower Show are always so expertly grown and perfectly arranged. This inspired me to make a quilt that geometrically showed some of the colorful flowers.

JEANNE WILLIAMSON
Natick, Massachusetts

FLOWER SHOW FLOWERS ARE ALWAYS PERFECT
40" x 41"

Brushed cotton, Deka® permanent fabric paint

Hand-stamped with rubber erasers on one piece of fabric, washed, machine-quilted

ERIKA CARTER
Bellevue, Washington

PARAMETERS: CHAOS
67.5" x 45"

Commercial cottons, hand-painted
silk organza, hand-painted cotton
muslin, Createx® paint

Hand-painted torn fabrics,
machine-appliquéd to muslin base,
machine-quilted

Parameters: Chaos is the second work in a series
about defining self in abstract, visual terms. In personal terms, it is a work about the tension and stress
I felt when our house was being painted and my
reaction to those stresses. Abstractly, the myriad of
squares and thin rectangles to the right and left of
the center suggest the power, creativity, and occa-
sional pattern inherent in chaos. It is human to
emphasize these elements and attempt to create
order out of chaos. The machine-stitched hands
amid the structured center squares further suggest
the human element in this structuring.

49

Parameters: Breakdown is the third work in a series about defining self in abstract visual terms. It is a work about redefining the parameters within which one can strive to succeed and grow. In this piece, the parameters no longer serve the self, and it is time to change, to break down old parameters and attempt to tap new energy as represented by the yellow margins.

ERIKA CARTER
Bellevue, Washington

PARAMETERS: BREAKDOWN
68" x 45"

Hand-painted cotton muslin,
hand-painted silk organza,
Createx® paint

Hand-painted torn fabrics,
machine-appliquéd to muslin base,
machine-quilted

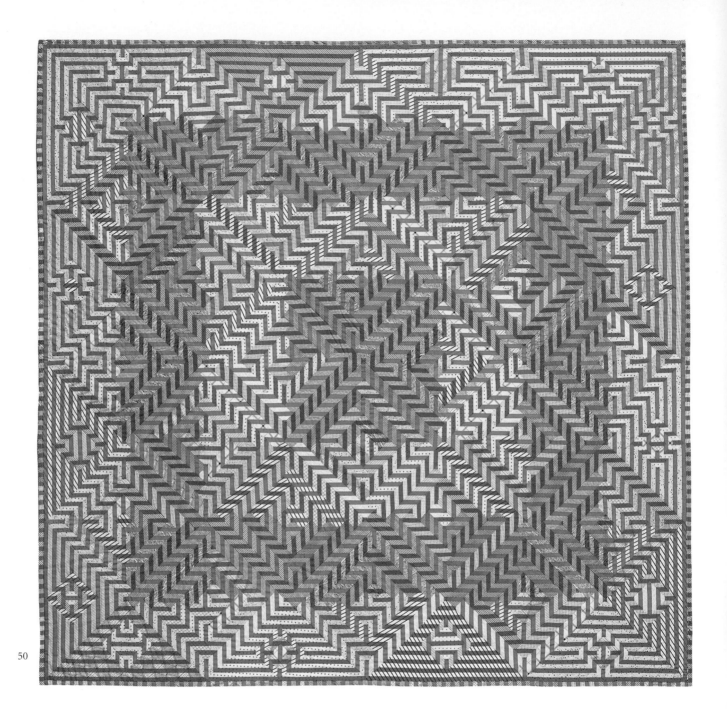

ELLEN OPPENHEIMER
Oakland, California

LOG CABIN MAZE
72" x 72"
Commercial fabrics that are hand-printed and overdyed

Machine-sewn, hand-quilted

I have always been fascinated with the Log Cabin design. I realized that I could adapt a Log Cabin block to make a Maze quilt. This quilt has a continuous line going through it—the yellow line in mathematical terms is a "continuous curve." In symbolic terms, this line represents the convoluted journeys that we take to get to exactly where we started.

My work on fabric with wax, dye, and wood block prints has been concurrent with some "body-work" or exercises about energy that I have studied and practiced. These exercises are based on ancient Chinese theories of how energy flows from the Earth through our bodies and can be exchanged with energy from other living things. I think the color and form in this quilt reflect that energy.

ANN M. ADAMS
San Antonio, Texas

RADIANT ENERGY
50" x 59"

Cotton broadcloth, fiber-reactive dye, pigments, metallic thread

Wax resist, block printed, discharge printed, machine-pieced, machine-appliquéd, machine-quilted

MELISSA HOLZINGER
Arlington, Washington

RED SKY IN THE MORNING
30.5" x 47.25"

Cotton duck, felt, acrylic paint, pastels, embroidery floss

Hand-painted, airbrushed, machine-embroidered, machine-pieced, machine-quilted

The world is bursting with information. Much of it is indecipherable due to its complexity, its seemingly contradictory nature, and its sheer mind-numbing immensity. How shall I read the signs? How shall I interpret the portents?

There is a nostalgic longing for the certainty and the clarity of childhood. There were simple adages to explain absolute truths. All the signs were understood because they were our very own. The glory of a fiery sky was simply that.

MELISSA HOLZINGER
Arlington, Washington

RED SKY AT NIGHT
29.5" x 48"

Cotton duck, acrylic paint, pastels, embroidery floss

Hand-painted, airbrushed, machine-embroidered, machine-pieced, machine-quilted

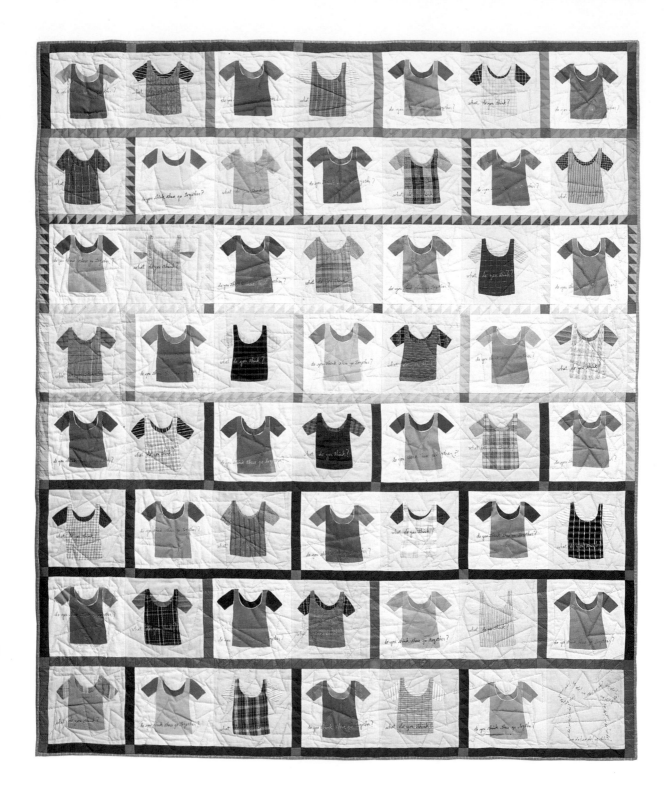

RACHEL BRUMER
Seattle, Washington

LET HER
61" x 72"

Cotton, fabric paints, polyester batting

Machine-pieced, hand-appliquéd, stenciled, hand-quilted

When my five-year-old daughter began kindergarten, she would come into my room in the morning after having dressed herself. She asked, "Does this go together?" I desperately wanted to say, "No! Solids with prints, not prints with prints. Pick out one of the colors in the print of the pants, and find a shirt that color." But no, I most often said, "What do you think?"

I woke up from a dream with this image. It was only a fragment of glowing color strips and warm light. The title of this quilt came from this dream image. Multicolored strips, which were cut without a straight edge, were interspersed with a variety of gray pieces. The horizonal bands and borders were also improvised. Machine quilting was done using various shades of gray and metallic threads.

CAROL M. MOE
Denver, Colorado

LUMEN I IMPROVISATION 493
73.5" x 60"

Cottons, Debra Lunn hand-dyed fabrics, cotton and metallic thread, cotton batting

Machine-pieced, machine-quilted

GRETCHEN ECHOLS
Seattle, Washington

BOB AND RITA TRY TO FORGET (DIPTYCH)
96" x 48"

Cotton, heat transfers of color images, ribbon, buttons, DMC® perle cotton, Cotton Classic® batting

Machine-pieced, machine-appliquéd, machine-quilted, hand-quilted

As a storyteller I present images the way they come in dreams, full of mystery and meaning. This work comments on men and women, masculine and feminine, my mother and father, humanity in general learning and forgetting the lessons of life.

Against the compartmentalized background of our lives we build tall towers for our most precious ideals. As we go about our daily lives attending to the mundane like men and women have through the ages we forget much of what we have learned about ourselves and each other as we focus on daily life and trying to avoid pain and suffering. We try to communicate to each other in the borderlands of our lives but much is garbled and backward. However, the legend of the phoenix and the renewal of spring remind us that rebirth is always present in the face of loss.

57

ROXANA BARTLETT
Boulder, Colorado

BETWEEN THE SPIRIT AND THE DUST
69" x 69"

Cotton sateen, cotton velvet, perle
cotton

Machine-pieced, dyed, painted,
appliquéd, tied

The transiency of lives and the poignancy of
inevitable goodbyes are the heart of my work. The
images arise spontaneously and are often triggered
by sights or feelings that may only last a moment—
but in that moment, all the joys and sorrows of life
come rushing in. As in a dream or memory of long
ago, the moment is more clearly felt than
understood.

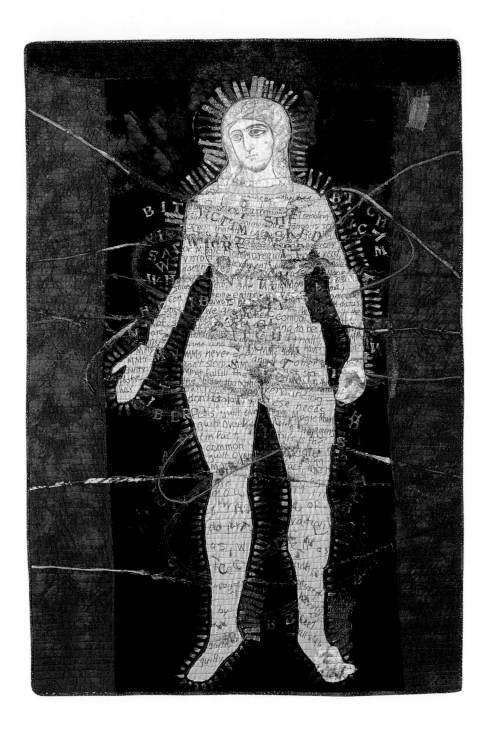

I created the figure of a woman using a photo transfer on voile of a 12th-century Russian icon as the head. This piece hung in my studio unadorned for six months while I thought about the differing roles women play and the invasions of women's self in our society. I then filled the body with words and images of what society does to women.

NANCY CONDON
Stillwater, Minnesota

BITCHES, VICTIMS, SAINTS, AND WHORES ONE: BOUNDARY VIOLATIONS
42" x 64"

Cotton, linen, fabric paint, fabric markers, acrylic paint

Machine-pieced, machine-appliquéd, machine-quilted

LIZ AXFORD
Houston, Texas

FREEHAND 8: TORN
70" x 53"

Cottons, hand-dyed cottons, cotton batting

Improvisationally pieced, machine-quilted

This is the fifth piece I've made using this block, an original variation of the traditional Log Cabin block. My palette began with a group of fabrics triple-dyed in varying strengths of red, gold, and green to produce a wide range of oranges, greens, and browns, some streaked, some rather even. Other colors from my collection of hand-dyed and commercial fabrics were added as I designed the quilt. The quilting design, inspired by Shoowa textiles, was improvised "freehand" at the sewing machine.

[Editor's Note: A detail of this quilt is on the front cover of this catalog.]

THE ARTISTS OF VISIONS: 1987-1992

■ VISIONS 1987:

Ann M. Albertson

Gerlinde Anderson

Denise Angioli

Sylvia Apple

Barbara Dee Baumgarten

Christine Beck

Judy Becker

Patty Bentley

Gail Binney-Winslow

Christal Carter

Barbara L. Crane

Mary Jo Dalrymple

Janet DeMars

LaVerne Domach

Sandra Townsend Donabed

Kathy Erickson

Caryl Bryer Fallert

Betty Ferguson

Marie Fritz

Darleen Fuller

Nancy Gadsby

Carol H. Gersen

Peggy Goetz

Kimberley Graf

Peg Hall

Sharon Heidingsfelder

Antoinette Holl

Betty E. Ives

Lynn Johnson

Marcia Karlin

Mary Laiuppa

Arlene Lane

Paula Lederkramer

Jean Lievens

Pat Magaret

Karen Maguire

Jane Malmgren

Carol McKie Manning

Mary Mashuta

Judy Mathieson

Anne H. Michener

Margaret J. Miller

Jo-Ann Murray

Joyce Murrin

Sara Nephew

Hallie H. O'Kelley

Marion Ongerth

Jan Patek

Charlotte Patera

Jean Pekarek

Mary Pyne

Donalene N. Rasmussen

Linda K. Sage

Janet Shore

Rebecca Simon

Patricia Brennan Smith

Becky Steinmetz

Marilyn Stothers

Eileen Bahring Sullivan

Juanita Swarts

Deborah B. Timby

Susan K. Turbak

Carol Ann Wadley

David Walker

Judy Anne Walter

Arlene Watters

Vickie Wilder

Joen Wolfrom

■ VISIONS 1990:
QUILTS OF A NEW DECADE

James Acord

Ann M. Adams

Carol Adleman

Charlotte Warr Andersen

Françoise Barnes

Joan Basore

Linda Liu Behar

Susan G. Bengtson

Sue Benner

Christen Brown

Gayle Bryan

Elizabeth A. Busch

Joyce Marquess Carey

Barbara Carow

Erika Carter

Carlene Chang

Stephanie Randall Cooper

Wendy Lewington Coulter

Barbara Lydecker Crane

Nancy Crasco

Lynn J. Crook

Deborah Ellen Davies

Gayle Earley

East Bay Heritage Quilters

Rosemary Elkes

Jean Evans

Caryl Bryer Fallert

Mary Fogg

Bobbie Fuhrmann

Ruth Garrison

Fiona Gavens

Carol H. Gersen

Helen Giddens

Alison Goss

Gail Hanson Greengard

Carol Anne Grotrian

Sandra K. Harrington

Sharon Heidingsfelder

Bonnie Bucknam Holmstrand

Inge Hueber

Marcia Karlin

Natasha Kempers-Cullen

Glenda L. King

Ann Kowaleski

Judith Larzelere

Susan Webb Lee

Linda Levin

Linda Ruth MacDonald

Marguerite Malwitz

Terrie Hancock Mangat

Merrill Mason

Kathleen H. McCrady

Ruth B. McDowell

Carol McKie Manning

Jeannette DeNicolis Meyer

Mary Morgan

Rachel Beth Mosler

Susan T. Mosler

Joyce Murrin

Jean Neblett Nägy

Katie Pasquini-Masopust

Sue Pierce

Lyn Piercy

Jane Reeves

Michiko Rice

Jane A. Sassaman

62 Joy Saville

Constance Scheele

Sally A. Sellers

Susan Shie

Carol Soderlund

Judy Sogn

Michiko Sonobe

Arlene Stamper

Glenne Stoll

Nancy Taylor

Bonny Tinling

Ann Trusty

Emily Zopf

■ VISIONS 1992:
THE ART OF THE QUILT

James Acord

Carol Adleman

Deirdre Amsden

Liz Axford

Joy Baaklini

Lisa Beaman

Judy Becker

Jeanne Benson

Karen Felicity Berkenfeld

Elizabeth A. Busch

Kathi Casey

Michael Cummings

Kathleen Deneris

Marilyn Dillard

Caryl Bryer Fallert

Jenifer Eveleth Fisher

Linda Fowler

Irena Goos

Kalia L. Hansen

Lynn C. Harper

Barbara Oliver Hartman

Sue Holdaway-Heys

Angela Holland

Melissa Holzinger

Judy Hooworth

Inge Hueber

Michael James

Melody Johnson

Reiko Kato

Carol Keller

Nobuko Kubota

M. Joan Lintault

Debra Lunn

Sumiko Maeda

Terrie Hancock Mangat

Mary Mashuta

Nina Morti

Jan Myers-Newbury

Miriam Nathan-Roberts

Jean Neblett

Velda Newman

Kathleen D. O'Connor

Marion Ongerth

Ellen Oppenheimer

Elizabeth Cherry Owen

Ruth Palmer

Sue Pierce

Anita Rabinoff-Goldman

Linda Kimura Rees

Emily Richardson

Janet Robinson

Rebecca Rohrkaste

Carol Rothrock

Chime Saltz

Junko Sawada

Alison Schwabe

Susan Shie

Jen Shurtliff

Catherine McConnell Stanton

Janet Steadman

Dorle Stern-Straeter

Mary Jo Stroh

Hana Tanaka

Meiny Vermaas-van der Heide

Judith Vierow

Carol Ann Wadley

David Walker

Coleen Walters

Noriko Watanabe

Nancy Whittington

Jeanne Williamson

Jason W. Yenter

INDEX

63

SPONSORS

We received significant help from these corporate sponsors in producing this catalog. We are very grateful for their financial assistance and their continued interest in promoting the quilt as art.

■ P&B TEXTILES

Creator of 100%-cotton prints and solids that inspire and fulfill the needs of quiltmakers worldwide

■ OMNIGRID®

Creating a Revolution in Rotary Cutting

A generous grant from Omnigrid has helped to make the traveling exhibition possible.

■ Rahr-West Art Museum, Manitowoc, Wisconsin

October 1 to November 26, 1995

■ Arkansas Arts Center, Little Rock, Arkansas

January 14 to February 28, 1996

■ NIHON VOGUE CO., LTD.

Nihon Vogue is the sponsor of the Quilts Japan Award. The objective of the Quilts Japan Award is to express gratefulness for the continued growth of the Japanese quilt, which is due greatly to American quilters, and to pay respect to the predecessors of quiltmaking. With this Award, Nihon Vogue hopes to play a role in the development of quiltmaking by helping to link the ties between Japanese and American quiltmakers. The winner of the 1994 Quilts Japan Award is Risë Nagin of Pittsburgh, Pennsylvania.

■ SOUTH SEA IMPORTS

Manufacturer of many fine quilting fabrics including the Mary Ellen Hopkins, Authentic Prints, and Sheryl/Roy collections.

Other Fine Quilting Books From C & T Publishing

An Amish Adventure, Roberta Horton
Appliqué 12 Easy Ways! Elly Sienkiewicz
Appliqué 12 Borders and Medallions, Elly Sienkiewicz
The Art of Silk Ribbon Embroidery, Judith Montano
Baltimore Album Quilts, Historic Notes and Antique Patterns, Elly Sienkiewicz
Baltimore Album Revival! Historic Quilts in the Making. The Catalog of C&T Publishing's Quilt Show and Contest, Elly Sienkiewicz
Baltimore Beauties and Beyond (2 Volumes), Elly Sienkiewicz
Calico and Beyond, Roberta Horton
Christmas Traditions From the Heart, Margaret Peters
Christmas Traditions From the Heart, Volume Two, Margaret Peters
A Colorful Book, Yvonne Porcella
Colors Changing Hue, Yvonne Porcella
Crazy Quilt Handbook, Judith Montano
Crazy Quilt Odyssey, Judith Montano
Design a Baltimore Album Quilt! Elly Sienkiewicz
Dimensional Appliqué—Baskets, Blooms & Borders, Elly Sienkiewicz
Fantastic Figures: Ideas & Techniques Using the New Clays, Susanna Oroyan
14,287 Pieces of Fabrics and Other Poems, Jean Ray Laury
Happy Trails, Pepper Cory
Heirloom Machine Quilting, Harriet Hargrave
Imagery on Fabric, Jean Ray Laury
Isometric Perspective, Katie Pasquini-Masopust
Landscapes & Illusions, Joen Wolfrom
The Magical Effects of Color, Joen Wolfrom
Mariner's Compass, Judy Mathieson
Mastering Machine Appliqué, Harriet Hargrave
Memorabilia Quilting, Jean Wells
The New Lone Star Handbook, Blanche Young and Helen Young Frost
Pattern Play, Doreen Speckmann
Pieced Clothing, Yvonne Porcella
Pieced Clothing Variations, Yvonne Porcella
Plaids and Stripes, Roberta Horton
Patchwork Quilts Made Easy, Jean Wells (co-published with Rodale Press, Inc.)
Quilts for Fabric Lovers, Alex Anderson
Quilts, Quilts, and More Quilts! Diana McClun and Laura Nownes
Stitching Free: Easy Machine Pictures, Shirley Nilsson
Story Quilts, Mary Mashuta
Symmetry: A Design System for Quiltmakers, Ruth B. McDowell
3 Dimensional Design, Katie Pasquini
A Treasury of Quilt Labels, Susan McKelvey
Virginia Avery's HATS, a Heady Affair
Virginia Avery's Nifty Neckwear
Visions: The Art of the Quilt, Quilt San Diego

For more information write for a free catalog from
C & T Publishing,
P.O. Box 1456
Lafayette, CA 94549
(1-800-284-1114)